INCOME MOBILITY IN THE U.S.:
EVIDENCE FROM INCOME TAX RETURNS
FOR 1987 AND 1996

by
Gerald E. Auten
and
Geoffrey Gee
U.S. Department of the Treasury

OTA Paper 99   **May 2007**

The OTA Papers Series is an occasional series of reports on the research, models, and datasets developed to inform and improve Treasury's tax policy analysis. The papers are works in progress and subject to revision. Views and opinions expressed are those of the authors and do not necessarily represent official Treasury positions or policy. OTA papers are distributed in order to document OTA analytic methods and data and invite discussion and suggestions for revision and improvement. Comments are welcome and should be directed to the authors.

Office of Tax Analysis
U.S. Treasury Department
Washington, D.C. 20220

The authors are grateful to Deena Ackerman, Leonard Burman, Jim Cilke, Julie-Anne Cronin, Robert Carroll, Geraldine Gerardi, Bradley Heim, Janet Holtzblatt, Donald Kiefer, William Randolph, Harvey Rosen and Eugene Steuerle for their helpful comments on prior drafts. The authors are also indebted to the Statistics of Income Division of the Internal Revenue Service and Jim Cilke for their work in developing the data sets used in this study. The views expressed in this paper are those of the authors and do not necessarily represent the views of the U.S. Treasury Department.

Abstract

There is considerable income mobility in the U.S. economy as households move up and down in the income distribution over time. Previous studies have typically found that roughly half of the families in the bottom 20 percent of the income distribution have moved up out of the bottom 20 percent within 10 years and that some of them have moved all the way to the top 20 percent. This paper examines income mobility in the United States during the period 1987 through 1996 using individual income tax data. The analysis uses three alternative measures of relative and absolute income mobility that provide different perspectives on changes in household income over time. Consistent with prior studies, this study finds significant household income mobility over this period. More than half (56 percent by one measure and 57 percent by another measure) of households moved to a higher or lower income quintile between 1987 and 1996. Approximately half (61 percent by one measure and 45 percent by another measure) of the households initially in the bottom 20 percent of the population moved to a higher quintile within ten years. In addition, this study finds that the largest percentage increases in real incomes were for those initially in the lowest income groups. The results illustrate how one-time snapshots of the income distribution provide only a partial picture of the economic situation of households by ignoring the effects of income mobility on the well-being of households over time.

Gerald Auten
Office of Tax Analysis
Main U.S. Treasury Building
Washington, D.C. 20220
gerald.auten@do.treas.gov

Geoffrey Gee
Office of Tax Analysis
Main U.S. Treasury Building
Washington, D.C. 20220
geoffrey.gee@do.treas.gov

Income Mobility in the U.S.: Evidence from Income Tax Returns

I.   Introduction

Many studies have documented the long-term trend of increasing income inequality in the U.S. economy. For example, U.S. Census data show that the share of household income of the top 20 percent of households increased from 44.1 percent in 1980 to 50.4 percent by 2005, with the share of the bottom 20 percent decreasing from 4.2 percent to 3.4 percent over this period.[1] Similarly, Piketty and Saez (1998, 2007) find that the share of income of the top 10 percent of taxpayers increased from 31.7 percent in 1960 to 44.3 percent in 2005, while the share of the top 1 percent increased from 8.4 percent to 17.4 percent.

Another important dimension of the analysis of income inequality, however, is the considerable movement of households – both up and down – through the income distribution over time. Hence, a one-time snapshot of the income distribution and comparisons of such snapshots in different years can be misleading. Research shows that the distribution of lifetime incomes is more equal than a one-time snapshot suggests because a household's relative position in the income distribution often changes over time. Concerns about income inequality in a particular year may be lessened to the extent that low incomes are temporary and income mobility provides individuals and families the opportunity to improve their economic situation over time. In addition, different policy prescriptions might be appropriate for assisting those who are persistently low-income as compared to those whose incomes are only temporarily low.

Scholars and policy analysts have drawn analogies between income mobility and escalators, ladders and hotels with rooms of varying quality.[2] For example, the escalator analogy views opportunity such that no matter which step a person starts on, he or she can move up by working hard and playing by the rules.[3] The ladder analogy places more responsibility for movement (up or down) on individual effort. The opportunity for upward mobility has been seen as a defining characteristic of the U.S. economy.[4]

Studies typically find that roughly half of families in the bottom 20 percent of the income distribution will have moved up out of the bottom 20 percent within 10 years and some of these

---

[1] U.S. Census Bureau (2006).

[2] Litan and Slemrod (1999) use the escalator analogy, while (McMurrer and Sawhill, 1996b) use the similar analogy of moving up and down the economic ladder. In climbing a ladder, however, all the progress is due to effort, while with an escalator, much of the movement comes from the escalator itself (e.g., economic growth). Economic historian Joseph Schumpeter compared the income distribution to a hotel—with rooms that are always occupied, but often by different people. Some rooms are luxurious, but others are small and shabby. Fairness requires an opportunity to change rooms, and that the luxurious ones are not always occupied by the same people. Mobility means that over time, individuals sometimes occupy luxurious rooms, but at other times are in the shabbier ones. The luxurious rooms are occupied by different people at different times. See Sawhill and Condon (1992) for more discussion of this analogy. Holtz-Eakin, et al., (2000) connect mobility with Horatio Alger stories.

[3] Litan and Slemrod (1999) state that "A defining ethic of America has long been that, no matter which step you first land on or how great the distance to the higher steps, you have a good shot at moving up if, as President Clinton has frequently said, 'you work hard and play by the rules.' "

[4] Litan and Slemrod (1999).

families will have moved all the way to the top 20 percent.[5] Furthermore, there are openings at the top as well: studies commonly show that nearly half of the families in the top 20 percent had not been there 10 years earlier.[6]

This paper examines income mobility in the United States using data from individual income tax returns for the period 1987 through 1996. In order to provide a more complete picture of income mobility, the analysis uses three alternative measures of income mobility that provide different perspectives on changes in household income over time. Consistent with prior studies, the data in this study show significant income mobility over this period. More than half (56 by one measure and 57 percent by another measure) of households moved to a higher or lower income quintile between 1987 and 1996. Approximately half (61 percent by one measure and 45 percent by another measure) of the households initially in the lowest income 20 percent of the population had moved to a higher quintile by 1996. Similarly, depending on the measure used, 30 to 40 percent of households in the top 20 percent in 1987 had moved to a lower income quintile by 1996. In addition, the study finds that largest increases in real incomes occurred among households initially in the lowest income groups. The results are examined for their sensitivity to different factors that may affect mobility, such as the life cycle of income and marital status.

The analysis in this paper includes a number of advantages over prior studies of income mobility. While most prior studies examine a single mobility measure, this study uses three alternative measures of income mobility so as to account for different aspects of mobility. In addition, the data set used in this study is substantially larger than those used in most prior studies, including a larger sample of high-income households. Finally, the study uses an improved measure of income over a 1992 Treasury study, a measure made possible by changes in tax law and improvements in data collection.

II.   Alternative Measures of Income Mobility

There are two basic types of measures of income mobility: relative income mobility measures and absolute income mobility measures.[7] Relative income mobility measures show how the income of households changes over time relative to the incomes of other households, while absolute income mobility measures show how the real incomes of households change over time. This study focuses on two measures of relative income mobility and one measure of absolute income mobility. Each of the measures has certain advantages and provides a different perspective on income mobility.

Both of the measures of relative income mobility are illustrated using a transition matrix that shows the movement of households across population quintiles (the lowest 20 percent, the

---

[5] For example, Bradbury and Katz (2002a) found that 46.7% of families in the bottom 20% of families in 1988 had moved out of the bottom 20% ten years later. Over 4 percent made it into the top 20%. Similarly, 46.8% of the families in the top 20% had not been there 10 years earlier. McMurrer and Sawhill (1996b) review other mobility studies that generally show similar results.

[6] For example, Sawhill and Condon (1992) report that 50 percent of families in the top quintile in 1986 had been in a lower quintile in 1977. Bradbury and Katz (2002) report that 46.8 percent of families in the top quintile in 1998 were in a lower quintile in 1988.

[7] Closely related measures include income variability over time and the correlation between income in one time period and income in another time period.

second 20 percent, etc). For households in each income quintile in the initial year, the transition matrix shows the percentages that end up in each income quintile in a later year. Results for the top 1, 5 and 10 percent of the population are also reported. The two measures differ, however, in the comparison group used in the ending year of the time period under examination.

The first measure of relative income mobility shows how the incomes of households change over a period of time relative to the incomes of all households in the population. In this measure, the income thresholds for determining the income quintiles are based on all comparable households in the population in both the initial and ending year. Thus, in this study, the income thresholds for 1987 are based on the full tax-filing population cross-section in 1987 while the income thresholds for 1996 are based on the full cross-section in 1996. Since this study examines only households where the primary taxpayer is age 25 or over, the income thresholds are based on the comparable age group in the full cross-section populations.

The second measure of relative income mobility compares how the incomes of households change over a time period relative to the incomes of that same group of households. In this measure, the income thresholds for determining the income quintiles in the initial and later year are based only on those households in the panel sample in both 1987 and 1996.

Absolute income mobility measures show how the real incomes of a group of households changes over time. Examples of such measures include the distribution of percentage increases or decreases in real (inflation-adjusted) income and movements into and out of poverty. The measure of absolute mobility used in this study shows how much the real income of households in each income quintile increased or decreased from 1987 to 1996. In particular, the measure shows the percent of households whose income increased by 5, 25, 50 or 100 percent, decreased by those percentages or remained relatively unchanged (within 5 percent).

Which of the measures is best? Each measure has advantages and disadvantages and highlights different aspects of mobility. Thus, this study examines all three of them to learn what each reveals about income mobility.

While the quintile transition matrices used to measure relative income mobility appear to be relatively easy to understand, there are several aspects to keep in mind. Some households that move across quintiles may have very small changes in real income. Other households may have much larger increases or decreases in real income, but remain in the same quintile, so their income movement is not observed. In addition, households in the bottom quintile cannot move down in the transition matrix even if their income decreases dramatically, and households in the top quintile cannot move up even if their income increases dramatically.[8]

Examining how much absolute incomes change over time helps address the limitations of transition matrices. With measures of absolute income mobility, it is possible to illustrate that income changes can be win-win situations in which real incomes are increasing in all income classes due to economic growth.[9] Measures of absolute income are preferable when people are

---

[8] See Bradbury and Katz (2002b) and U.S. Treasury (1992b) for additional discussion of mobility measures.
[9] Of course, the reverse may apply during periods of recession or economic decline as real incomes could decline in all income classes.

more concerned about improving their own situation than about whether they are doing better than others. Such measures might be considered more closely associated with the notion that economic growth is a group process in which it is possible for everyone to come out ahead.

III.   Prior Studies of Income Mobility

While less is known about income mobility than about changes in inequality, beginning in the 1990s a number of studies examined various aspects of income mobility.[10] Sawhill and Condon (1992) used the Panel Study of Income Dynamics (PSID) to examine the mobility of individuals between the ages of 25 and 54 for the periods 1967-1976 and 1977-1986. Using the first measure of relative mobility that compares households within the panel, they found that over 60 percent of individuals were in a different family income quintile a decade later. Among individuals initially in the lowest income quintile, 44 percent moved to a higher quintile between 1967 and 1976 and 47 percent moved to a higher quintile between 1977 and 1986. Downward mobility from the top quintile was experienced by 47 and 50 percent in the two periods, respectively. A later study by McMurrer and Sawhill (1996b) concluded that mobility rates had remained unchanged in these two time periods.

Two 1992 Treasury studies (1992a and 1992b) examined mobility during the period 1979-1988 using a panel of 14,351 income tax returns and measuring income using constant-law measure of income as reported on income tax returns.[11] The Treasury data showed that 86 percent of taxpayers in the lowest income quintile in 1979 had moved to a higher quintile by 1988 and 15 percent of them had moved all the way to the top quintile. Among those who were in the top quintile in 1979, 65 percent were still there in 1988, and only 1 percent had dropped to the lowest quintile. The high mobility resulted from several features of the analysis. When the sample was limited to taxpayers age 25 to 64 and compared to taxpayers in the panel (i.e., the second relative mobility measure) rather than to all taxpayers aged 25 to 64, the Treasury data showed that 50 percent of the lowest income quintile had moved to a higher quintile after 10 years.[12] Thus, the results were very similar to Sawhill and Condon when a comparable sample and mobility measure were used.

Burkhauser, et.al.(1997) compared earnings mobility in the U.S. and Germany and found similar patterns in both countries. Their analysis showed that in the U.S., 45 percent of those in the lowest earnings quintile had moved to a higher quintile after five years. In addition, 46 percent of men and 50 percent of women moved up or down at least one earnings quintile after five years.

Bradbury and Katz (2002a, 2002b) used PSID data to examine relative income mobility in the 1970s, 1980s and 1990s. Their results show that about half of households in the bottom quintile

---

[10] McMurrer and Sawhill (1996a) summarize a number of the early mobility studies.

[11] The 1992 Treasury studies limited the sample to taxpayers who had filed in all 10 years from 1979 to 1988. Income was defined as real constant law adjusted gross income (AGI). This measure includes capital gains, but excludes Social Security benefits because they were not taxable until 1984 and thus no data were available for earlier years. For a more detailed description of constant law AGI see U.S. Treasury (1992a). Income percentiles for each year were computed using the full IRS Statistics of Income cross-section samples, which represent the full population of tax returns filing each year.

[12] See U.S. Treasury (1992b).

moved out after 10 years (51% for 1969-79, 50% for 1979-1989, 47% for 1988-98). The percent of the lowest quintile moving all the way to the top quintile increased slightly from 3 percent to 4 percent. They argue that the data show that relative mobility declined in the 1990s. They also show that the income gaps widened over this period, which would make mobility across quintiles more difficult. This widening of the income gap may account for the small decline in relative mobility.[13]

Carroll, Joulfaian and Rider (2006) examined the relative mobility of taxpayers initially age 30 to 50 over the period 1979 to 1995 using a panel of income tax returns. They found that 54 percent of tax households in the lowest quintile in 1979 had moved to a higher quintile in 1995 and about 4 percent reached the top quintile. Of those in the top income quintile in 1979, 47 percent had moved to a lower quintile by 1995. Only 30 percent of those in the top 1 percent in 1979 remained in the top 1 percent by 1995. They also found that mobility is greater in the middle three income quintiles than for those initially in the top or bottom quintile.

IV.   Data

The data for this study are from a 10-year panel of a sample of individual income tax returns for the years 1987 through 1996. The panel is based on a stratified random sample of approximately 88,000 tax returns for tax year 1987 and includes the tax returns of these taxpayers through tax year 1996.[14] Most of the tables for this study use the returns of taxpayers who filed in both 1987 and 1996.[15] To avoid counting transitions from school to work as mobility, the analysis follows the common practice in previous studies of excluding taxpayers under the age of 25 in the initial year.[16] The analysis in this study is based on households as defined for income tax purposes, which differs in some cases from households as defined for Census studies and in various surveys.[17] Since the definitions of income tax units and households are the same in most cases, this study uses the term households in describing the family units reflected on the income tax returns.

---

[13] It is unclear whether absolute mobility increased or decreased in these data as this study does not examine absolute income mobility. Table 1 in Bradbury and Katz (2002b) shows that average real incomes of families in the lowest quintile in 1988 increased from 1988 to 1998 after declining in the previous two decades, which may suggest some increase in absolute mobility.

[14] This panel excludes dependent filers and is described more completely in Cilke, et.al. (2001) and Ackerman, et.al. (forthcoming 2007). The original sample is supplemented by a refreshment sample that represents new non-dependent individuals and households who file in years after 1987.

[15] In order to include the largest sample, the analysis does not require that households file in all 10 years. Thus, households that did not file in interim years because their income fell below filing thresholds or for other reasons were not excluded.

[16] For example, Sawhill and Condon (1992) examine individuals aged of 25 and 54. A later section of the current study examines mobility when individuals over age 55 are excluded.

[17] Surveys generally define households as including all persons who occupy a housing unit, regardless of whether they are related, and include the income of all members of the household over 14 years of age. Income tax returns are filed by individuals or married couples filing jointly. Taxpayers may claim personal exemptions or tax credits for eligible dependents that in some cases, such as college students, may reside elsewhere. The income of dependents is generally not included on tax returns of parents, but those dependents may be required to file their own tax returns if income exceeds threshold amounts. See U.S. Treasury (1992b).

The primary measure of income used for the analysis is cash income and supplemented by data from information returns filed with the IRS and certain Social Security information. This is a comprehensive income measure that includes wages and salaries, dividends, taxable and tax-exempt interest, rental income, income from businesses and farms, taxable and non-taxable pensions, Social Security benefits (including the non-taxable portion), unemployment compensation, capital gains, gambling income, and other income reported on tax returns. The cash income measure used in this study is similar to cash income used in other studies. One difference is that some forms of transfer payments are not subject to tax and are thus not included. This is a limitation of using tax data and means that the incomes of some low-income households would be understated and that such households would be less likely to file a tax return. Nevertheless, the availability of comprehensive data on non-taxable Social Security benefits for all recipients means that the income measure captures about 84 percent of all cash transfer payments. Another difference is the inclusion of realized capital gains in the tax data used by this study, which typically are not reported in other data sources.[18]

As an additional comparison, the shares of cash income earned in each income quintile were calculated in 1987 and 1996 and found to be similar to other analyses. In the tax data, the share of income reported by the top quintile increased from 49.9 percent in 1987 to 54.0 percent in 1996, while the share of income of the lowest income quintile fell from 3.8 percent to 3.5 percent.[19] By comparison, in the Census data for this period, the share of income reported by the top quintile increased from 46.2 to 49.0 percent and the share of the lowest income quintile declined from 3.8 to 3.6 percent.[20] Thus the cross-section income distribution measures were similar in the Census data and the tax data, even though the Census measure does not include capital gains.

Since the data for this study are limited to households who file income tax returns, an important question is the extent to which the panel data accurately represents the total population. The lack of information on the income of non-filers is a limitation of the use of tax data. While taxpayers with incomes below certain thresholds are not required to file, these filing thresholds are relatively low. For tax year 1987, for example, the filing thresholds were $4,440 for single taxpayers and heads of households under age 65, and $7,560 for married couples. By comparison, the poverty levels in 1987 were $5,909 for a single taxpayer under age 65, $7,829 for a head of household with one child under age 18, and $7,606 for a married couple under age 65 with no dependents. This means that many households under the poverty level are required to file a tax return, and others do so in order to claim refundable tax credits or refunds of tax withheld. As a result, the number of primary and secondary taxpayers equaled 85.4 percent of the U.S. resident population for those age 25 and over and 92.5 percent of the U.S. resident

---

[18] It is important to note that the measure of income used in this study is broader than income measures generally used in previous mobility studies using tax return data. The most important differences are the inclusion of realized capital gains, tax-exempt interest and Social Security benefits. (including taxpayers below the income threshold at which Social Security benefits become taxable). The issue of taxable and non-taxable cash transfer payments is examined in more detail in the Technical Appendix.

[19] These computations were done including the refreshment sample to ensure that the comparisons accurately reflect the cross-section populations in both 1987 and 1996.

[20] U.S. Census Bureau (2006), Table A3. The Census data uses a measure of money income that includes additional sources of non-taxable transfer income and excludes capital gains, but is otherwise similar to the cash income measure used in this study.

population for those age 25 to 65. Thus, the tax 1987 tax-filing population was largely representative of the overall U.S. population between the ages of 25 and 64.[21] The tax filing population is less representative of the overall U.S. population for individuals under age 25 or age 65 and over as the filing rates are significantly lower in these age groups.[22] Tax data do not include some low-income and non-compliant households, however.

V.   Income Mobility of Households, 1987 to 1996

Table 1 shows how the incomes of households in different income groups in 1987 changed relative to the incomes of all households in the population in 1996. The income thresholds in 1987 and 1996 for the income quintile groups in this table are based on all households in the full cross-section populations in those two years where the primary taxpayer was age 25 and over. The table clearly shows the high degree of income mobility over this period. Over 61 percent of households (i.e., $61.1 = 100 - 38.9$) in the lowest income quintile moved up to a higher quintile by 1996. While 28 percent moved up to the second quintile, over 7 percent moved all the way to the top quintile. While households in the top quintile had a higher probability of staying there in 1996, about one-third (32 percent) had dropped to a lower quintile. More than half (54 percent) of the top 1 percent of households in 1987 had dropped to a lower income group by 1996. Another way of looking at this is that more than half of the households in the top 1 percent in 1996 were not there nine years earlier. This is notable because some editorials and articles in the press about the increasing income shares of the top 1 percent may induce the casual reader to conclude that the incomes of a fixed group of households is receiving this larger share. About one-third of the households in the middle income quintile in 1987 were still in the middle quintile in 1996. Almost twice as many (42.6 percent = 28.4 +14.2) had moved to a higher income class by 1996 than dropped to a lower quintile (23.5 percent = 6.1 +17.4). While not shown directly in the table, 57.1 percent of the households filing tax returns in 1987 had moved to a different income quintile in 1996.[23]

---

[21] Some taxpayers in the original sample dropped out of the filing population due to death, emigration, falling below the filing threshold, or failing to file for some other reason, this panel represents a declining portion of the tax filing population over time. An attrition table in the Technical Appendix shows overall attrition of about 16 percent of the original sample, about half of which was due to the death of the primary taxpayer.

[22] The Technical Appendix includes a more detailed analysis of the relationship of the tax filing population to the total resident U.S. population.

[23] This is calculated by summing all of the non-diagonal cells and dividing this number by 5. The diagonal cells contain households in the same quintile in both years. The division by 5 adjusts for the fact that the percentages in each quintile row sum to 100 percent, or 500 percent for all five rows.

Table 1: Income Mobility Relative to the Total Tax Filing Population, Age 25 and Over, 1987-1996

1987 Income Quintile	1996 Income Quintile						Top 10%	Top 5%	Top 1%
	Lowest	Second	Middle	Fourth	Highest	Total			
Lowest	38.9	28.3	14.9	10.6	7.3	100.0	3.4	1.7	0.3
Second	14.2	33.8	26.4	16.4	9.3	100.0	3.2	1.2	0.2
Middle	6.1	17.4	33.9	28.4	14.2	100.0	5.6	2.3	0.3
Fourth	3.0	7.5	19.4	40.1	30.0	100.0	10.3	3.8	0.5
Highest	1.8	2.5	7.3	20.6	67.8	100.0	42.6	23.9	5.4
Top 10%	1.8	1.5	4.4	13.6	78.7	100.0	60.6	38.9	9.9
Top 5%	1.9	1.4	3.2	8.2	85.2	100.0	73.3	56.3	17.3
Top 1%	2.1	0.9	2.5	4.7	89.9	100.0	83.3	75.8	46.0
All	11.3	16.5	20.1	24.1	28.0	100.0	14.4	7.3	1.5

Source: U.S. Treasury Department, 1987-1996 Family Panel.
Notes: The rows sum to 100 percent across the five quintiles in the first five columns. The table includes returns of households who filed for both 1987 and 1996 where the primary taxpayer is age 25 or over in 1987. The income levels for the quintiles and top percentiles in 1987 and 1996 are determined for the full cross-sections of tax returns for 1987 and 1996 respectively, where the primary taxpayer is age 25 and over. Income is cash income as defined in the text and the technical appendix.

The bottom row of Table 1 illustrates that overall, households present in the 1987 population have moved up in the income distribution by 1996. Only 11.3 percent of the households who filed returns in 1987 are in the bottom quintile of the total tax filing population in 1996, while 28.0 percent are in the top quintile and 24.1 percent are in the second quintile. This upward movement reflects the fact that new entrants into the age 25 and over population are more likely to enter with below average incomes. In part, this reflects life cycle income patterns as newly entering young households initially have low incomes but their incomes increase more rapidly. It also reflects the fact that new immigrants are more likely to enter the population with lower incomes. The extent of the overall upward movement of the 1987 population may seem surprising in that the table includes the downward movement of incomes of older households whose incomes commonly decline after retirement.[24]

Table 2 shows the income mobility of households in 1987 relative to those same households in 1996. Note that unlike Table 1, the construction of this table means that in the bottom row showing all households, 20 percent of the 1987 households are in each of the 1996 quintiles.[25] Since no new lower-income households enter the comparison population in this table, there is no overall upward movement of the 1987 households within the overall income distribution. Thus, it is more difficult for households in the bottom quintile to rise in the relative distribution. Nevertheless, almost half of the lowest income quintile (45.4 percent) moved to a higher quintile by 1996. Overall mobility was approximately the same as in the first mobility measure as 56

---

[24] Table 4 in the following section shows mobility when households where the primary taxpayer is age 65 and over are omitted from the analysis. Income mobility out of the lowest income is slightly greater when the older group is omitted, while downward mobility out of the top quintile is slightly lower. Table 6 shows that the real incomes of younger households generally increased, while those of older households declined.

[25] This is because Table 2 is constructed by classifying the same group of tax households based on their 1987 income and then by income percentiles based on their 1996 income. There are no additional young or new immigrant households against which the incomes of these households are being compared as in Table 1.

percent of households moved to a higher or lower income quintile. As compared to Table 1, this measure of relative income mobility implies more downward mobility.[26] For example, a smaller portion of the 1987 top quintile remained in the top quintile in 1996, 58 percent as compared to 68 percent in Table 1. More than half of the households in the top 1 percent in 1987 (54 percent) dropped out of the top 1 percent by 1996, although 90 percent of them remained in the top quintile.

Table 2: Income Mobility Relative to the Panel Population, Age 25 and Over, 1987-1996

1987 Income Quintile	1996 Income Quintile							Top 10%	Top 5%	Top 1%
	Lowest	Second	Middle	Fourth	Highest	Total				
Lowest	54.6	22.1	11.1	7.5	4.7	100.0		2.2	1.1	0.2
Second	25.5	36.5	20.3	12.0	5.7	100.0		2.0	0.6	0.2
Middle	12.0	24.6	32.9	19.9	10.6	100.0		4.2	1.7	0.3
Fourth	5.1	12.3	25.0	37.0	20.5	100.0		6.8	2.7	0.3
Highest	2.7	4.6	10.8	23.5	58.4	100.0		34.8	18.9	4.1
Top 10%	2.5	3.0	6.7	14.9	72.9	100.0		52.9	31.5	7.6
Top 5%	2.5	2.4	4.6	9.6	80.9	100.0		67.1	47.5	13.5
Top 1%	2.5	1.6	3.5	6.1	86.3	100.0		80.0	71.6	38.1
All	20.0	20.0	20.0	20.0	20.0	100.0		10.0	5.0	1.0

Source: U.S. Treasury Department, 1987-1996 Family Panel.
Notes: The rows sum to 100 percent across the five quintiles in the first five columns. The table includes returns of households that filed for both 1987 and 1996 where the primary taxpayer is age 25 or over in 1987. The income thresholds for the quintiles and top percentiles in 1987 and 1996 are determined using only the returns of taxpayers in the panel who filed in both years. Income is cash income as defined in the text and the technical appendix.

The third approach examines absolute income mobility. This approach measures whether households were better or worse off over time, and by how much. As shown in Table 3, over half of the households (54.7 percent) increased their real incomes by 5 percent or more between 1987 and 1996, and median household income increased by 11.1 percent.[27] Increases in real income were the largest for households with the lowest incomes in 1987.[28] Among households in the lowest income quintile in 1987, the median income increased 80.6 percent by 1996. Real incomes increased by at least 5 percent over the period for 77 percent of these low-income households and at least doubled for almost half of this group. Among households in the highest income quintile in 1987, income increased by at least 5 percent for 40.5 percent of households in the top quintile and doubled for only 7.5 percent of households. The median income of those in

---

[26] The greater downward mobility results from the construction of Table 2 because for every household that moves up another must move down. The table construction combined with the fact discussed previously that new entrants into the population have lower incomes on average produces the result of more downward mobility using this measure.

[27] By comparison, in the U.S. Census data (2006), median household real income increased by 2.7 percent from $42,827 to $43,967 in 2005 CPI-U-RS adjusted dollars. The difference is that the Census data measures changes in the full cross-section population including new entrants, while the data in Table 3 show changes in incomes of households that filed income tax returns in 1987.

[28] A recent CBO study (May 2007) reported that the average income of households with children in the lowest income quintile in 2005 was 35 percent higher than the average income of comparable households in 1991. As the CBO report makes clear, the CBO finding does not describe changes for individual households over time. Table 3 complements the CBO analysis by following individual households over time.

the top quintile in 1987 declined by 1.8 percent, while the median income of those in the top 1 percent in 1987 declined by 23.8 percent. While this study does not examine these results in detail, contributing factors may include declines in incomes after retirement and "mean reversion" in which the incomes of households whose incomes were temporarily high in 1987 revert to a level closer to their long-run average.

Among households in the middle income quintile in 1987, median income increased by 9.1 percent. Real incomes increased by at least 5 percent for 53 percent of households in this group and at least doubled for 11 percent. These results demonstrate that over the 1987 to 1996 period, incomes rose for the majority of households, and that upward income mobility was the greatest among those that began the period in the lowest income groups.

Table 3: Were Households Better Off? Absolute Income Mobility 1987-1996, Households Age 25 and Over

1987 Income	Ratio of 1996 Real Income to 1987 Income						Percent Change in:	
	Less than 0.50	0.50 to 0.95	No change	1.05 to 1.50	1.50 to 2.00	2.00 and over	Mean Income	Median Income
Lowest	8.7	10.3	4.0	17.0	12.8	47.3	247.5	80.6
Second	6.0	22.0	8.7	28.0	14.8	20.6	53.9	22.1
Middle	7.0	29.2	10.7	28.7	13.2	11.2	30.9	9.1
Fourth	8.1	34.5	10.2	30.9	9.6	6.6	15.6	2.3
Highest	14.2	36.3	9.1	25.6	7.4	7.5	9.6	-1.8
Top 10%	18.0	34.7	8.1	22.6	7.6	8.9	10.3	-4.0
Top 5%	23.2	31.7	6.5	20.3	8.0	10.2	9.4	-8.2
Top 1%	37.0	26.7	4.8	14.3	6.6	10.7	1.6	-23.8
All	9.0	27.6	8.8	26.4	11.3	17.0	24.1	11.1

Source: U.S. Treasury Department, 1987-1996 Family Panel.
Notes: The rows sum to 100 percent across columns 1 to 8. The table includes returns of households who filed for both 1987 and 1996 where the primary taxpayer is age 25 or over in 1987. Income is cash income as defined in the text and the technical and data appendix.

While each of the measures of mobility illustrates a different perspective on income mobility, all of the measures demonstrate the high degree of income mobility in the U.S. However, they do not provide information on the factors that affect mobility. For example, the income mobility in these measures includes income changes resulting from changes in marital status or retirement. The following sections consider the effects of these and other factors on the measurement of income mobility.

VI.   Sensitivity Testing and Income Mobility Across Population Subgroups

Since measurement of income mobility can be sensitive to the specific features of the analysis such as the definition of income, the treatment of changes in marital status, and the population groups examined, this section reports a number of sensitivity tests of alternative assumptions. To keep the number of tables within reasonable bounds, most of the sensitivity tests are compared to Table 1 (mobility relative to the total tax filing population in 1996) where possible. The first sensitivity test was to redo Table 1 with an alternative definition of income that omits capital gains. The realization of capital gains income from the sale of stock or other assets is generally voluntary and can be irregular or bunched over time. In addition, some survey measures of cash income do not include capital gains or may not measure them well. Thus, some of the apparent mobility in Table 1 could simply reflect the bunching of capital gains. When the alternative measure of income was used, however, the resulting table was virtually the same as Table 1, with no cell changing more than 0.2 percent. We conclude that capital gains did not affect the mobility results, and therefore do not show these results separately.[29]

Income mobility is partly determined by factors related to the life cycle, including faster income growth of new entrants to the workforce (e.g., college graduates obtaining their first job) and income declines when people exit from the workforce (e.g., retirement). Thus, it is useful to examine the sensitivity of the mobility results to the age limits imposed on the sample population. Table 4 shows income mobility first when the sample is restricted to households age 25 through 55 in 1987 and Table 5 shows mobility when the sample is expanded to include taxpayers of all ages, including non-dependent taxpayers under the age of 21. The income thresholds are determined in the same way as in Table 1, that is, by reference to the full tax filing population of the relevant age groups in 1987 and 1996.

In general, changing the age limits of the sample of household has only modest effects on measured mobility and in the direction one would expect. When the relevant population is restricted to households age 25 to 55 in 1987 (the oldest would be age 64 by 1996), income mobility out of the bottom quintile increases slightly from 61 percent to 65 percent. Households in the top quintile are slightly more likely to remain in the top quintile (71 percent compared to 68 percent in Table 1). These differences are likely due to the omission of older households whose income declines due to retirement from the labor force.

Table 4: Income Mobility Relative to the Total Population for Households Age 25-55, 1987-1996

1987 Income Quintile	1996 Income Quintile							Top 10%	Top 5%	Top 1%
	Lowest	Second	Middle	Fourth	Highest	Total				
Lowest	35.4	29.5	16.8	11.0	7.4	100.0		3.3	1.8	0.3
Second	12.6	29.4	28.8	18.8	10.4	100.0		3.6	1.4	0.2
Middle	5.7	13.6	30.7	32.7	17.3	100.0		7.0	3.0	0.4
Fourth	2.9	5.8	15.3	40.7	35.4	100.0		12.4	4.6	0.6
Highest	1.9	2.2	6.4	18.4	71.1	100.0		46.0	26.2	5.9
Top 10%	1.9	1.4	3.7	11.8	81.3	100.0		64.3	42.6	11.1
Top 5%	2.2	1.2	2.3	7.1	87.3	100.0		77.6	62.0	20.0
Top 1%	2.1	1.0	1.4	3.4	92.1	100.0		88.3	81.3	51.9
All	10.9	15.4	19.4	24.8	29.5	100.0		15.1	7.8	1.6

Source: U.S. Treasury Department, 1987-1996 Family Panel.
Notes: The table includes returns of households who filed for both 1987 and 1996 where the primary taxpayer is age 25 to 55 in 1987. The income levels for the quintiles and top percentiles in 1987 and 1996 are determined using the

---

[29] While capital gains were unusually high in 1986 (7.4 percent of GDP) and in 1999 (6.0 percent of GDP), they were 3.1 percent of GDP in 1987 and 3.3 percent of GDP in 1996. Therefore realized capital gains were at similar levels in both years used in this study and at somewhat lower levels than in the years before 1986 and after 1996. For additional data on capital gains, see the Capital Gains tables on the U.S. Treasury Department website.

full cross-sections of tax returns for 1987 and 1996 respectively, where the primary taxpayer is age 25 to 55. Income is cash income as defined in the text and the technical appendix.

As shown in Table 5, mobility out of the bottom quintile is higher (71 percent versus 61 percent in Table 1) when the sample population is expanded to include households of all ages, but income mobility in the top quintile remains the same as in Table 1. This increase in measured mobility reflects the inclusion of younger individuals and families whose incomes are rising relatively rapidly as they move up quickly to better paying jobs or make the change from part-time work while a student to full-time employment.

Table 5: Income Mobility Relative to the Total Population for All Ages, 1987-1996

1987 Income Quintile	1996 Income Quintile						Top 10%	Top 5%	Top 1%
	Lowest	Second	Middle	Fourth	Highest	Total			
Lowest	29.1	27.4	18.9	15.4	9.1	100.0	3.9	1.7	0.3
Second	12.7	30.4	26.9	19.4	10.7	100.0	3.8	1.3	0.2
Middle	5.4	15.8	33.8	29.4	15.6	100.0	6.1	2.5	0.4
Fourth	2.6	7.0	19.6	40.8	30.0	100.0	10.6	4.1	0.5
Highest	1.5	2.0	6.9	21.5	68.0	100.0	42.2	23.4	5.2
Top 10%	1.4	1.4	4.1	14.0	79.1	100.0	60.3	38.3	9.6
Top 5%	1.7	1.2	3.1	8.7	85.3	100.0	73.1	56.1	16.7
Top 1%	1.8	0.9	2.4	5.0	90.0	100.0	84.0	75.6	45.8
All	9.6	15.5	20.7	25.7	28.5	100.0	14.4	7.2	1.5

Source: U.S. Treasury Department, 1987-1996 Family Panel.
Notes: The rows sum to 100 percent across the five quintiles in the first five columns. The table includes returns of all households who filed for both 1987 and 1996 regardless of age. The income levels for the quintiles and top percentiles in 1987 and 1996 are determined on the all tax returns in 1987 and 1996 respectively. Income is cash income as defined in the text and the technical appendix.

The more rapid growth of the real incomes of younger households and the effects of the life cycle on incomes are shown in Figure 1 and Table 6 below. Median real income increased 44 percent for households where the primary taxpayer was age 25 to 34 in 1987. The older the age group, the lower the median income change over this period. Median income rose 12 percent for households age 35 to 44 in 1987. Median real incomes declined 7 percent for households age 45 to 54, 16 percent for households age 55 to 64 and 8.8 percent for households age 65 and over in 1987. These income declines reflect the transition of households in these groups into retirement with wage and self-employment income being replaced by pension and Social Security income. The table also illustrates life cycle income patterns.[30] While the median income of the age 25 to 34 population cohort was below the median of the sample population in 1987, by 1996 the median income was higher than for the full sample population. The cohort age 45 to 54 in 1987 had the highest median income in that year, but by 1996 the median income of this group had declined below that of the two younger age groups. As discussed earlier, these results help to explain the absolute income mobility results in Table 3. The decline in income of households in

---

[30] The median incomes in Table 6 are calculated using the tax panel of households who filed returns in both 1987 and 1996 so as to show changes in income by age group. These medians are not the same as the median incomes of the full cross-section populations in these age groups in each year. Nevertheless, the table provides a rough measure of life cycle patterns as well as the income change of 1987 households by age group.

the top income quintile in 1987 reported in Table 3 is likely related to life cycle income patterns. The highest income quintile in any given year includes many households in their peak earnings years, while the lower income quintiles include many younger households whose peak earnings years are still ahead of them.

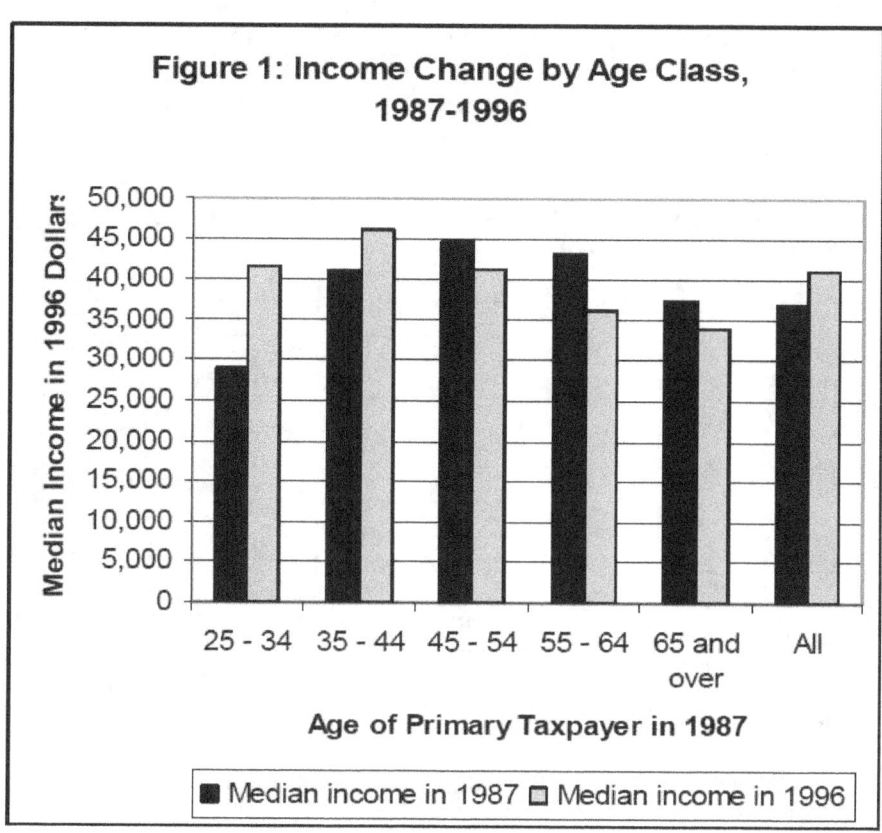

Figure 1: Income Change by Age Class, 1987-1996

Table 6: Income Change by Age Class, 1987-1996

Age Group in 1987	Median Income in 1987	Median Income in 1996	Median percent income	Mean Income in 1987	Mean Income in 1996	Mean percent income change
25 - 34	28,839	41,492	43.9	34,486	55,288	60.3
35 - 44	41,082	46,121	12.3	51,344	66,462	29.4
45 - 54	44,545	41,322	-7.2	59,120	65,834	11.4
55 - 64	43,248	36,213	-16.3	62,087	58,723	-5.4
65 and over	37,295	34,017	-8.8	57,880	53,061	-8.3
All	36,891	41,000	11.1	48,704	60,436	24.1

Source: U.S. Treasury Department, 1987-1996 Family Panel.
Notes: Income in 1987 is converted to 1996 dollars using the CPI-RS. This table includes all returns present in both 1987 and 1996 where the primary taxpayer is age 25 and over in 1987, except for returns of dependent filers. Age groups are based on the age of the primary taxpayer. Income is cash income as defined in the text and the technical appendix.

Another source of income mobility is changes in marital status. The effects of such changes in family status can be handled in several ways. Table 7 shows income mobility when the sample population is limited to those whose marital status is unchanged between 1987 and 1996. They are either married filing jointly in both years or not married in either year. Focusing on the population with unchanged marital status eliminates households where the mobility that results from divorce or from getting married and thus potentially having additional sources of income in the household.[31] Measured mobility out of the bottom quintile is about 11 percent lower (54 percent to 61 percent). In other words, about 11 percent of the observed income mobility out of the bottom income quintile appears to be due to individuals who get married and either have two incomes or a higher earning spouse. Downward mobility out of the top quintile is about 9 percent lower once marital status changes are taken out.

Table 7: Income Mobility of Households with Unchanged Marital Status Relative to the Total Tax Filing Population, Age 25 and Over, 1987-1996

1987 Income Quintile	1996 Income Quintile								
	Lowest	Second	Middle	Fourth	Highest	Total	Top 10%	Top 5%	Top 1%
Lowest	45.9	30.8	13.7	6.2	3.5	100.0	1.9	1.1	0.2
Second	15.9	39.5	29.0	12.0	3.7	100.0	1.3	0.6	0.1
Middle	5.9	17.6	38.0	28.8	9.6	100.0	3.2	1.2	0.1
Fourth	2.1	6.4	19.7	43.1	28.7	100.0	8.3	2.9	0.4
Highest	1.3	1.9	6.4	20.1	70.4	100.0	43.9	24.1	5.4
Top 10%	1.4	1.1	3.9	12.8	80.9	100.0	62.5	39.7	9.9
Top 5%	1.7	1.1	2.9	7.9	86.4	100.0	74.8	57.2	17.3
Top 1%	1.8	0.8	2.4	4.8	90.2	100.0	83.8	76.2	46.3
All	11.6	16.7	20.6	23.6	27.5	100.0	14.2	7.3	1.5

Source: U.S. Treasury Department, 1987-1996 Family Panel.
Notes: This table includes households who filed tax returns for both 1987 and 1996 where the primary taxpayer is age 25 or over in 1987 and where marital status was the same in both years. The income levels for the quintiles and top percentiles in 1987 and 1996 are determined using the full cross-section of tax returns in 1987 and 1996 respectively, where the primary taxpayer is age 25 and over. Income is cash income as defined in the text and the technical appendix.

One limitation of household analysis is that single individuals and married couples are counted the same in measuring income and determining the income quintiles.[32] Some studies have addressed this issue by using a measure of household equivalent income that adjusts for differences in household size. There are many measures of equivalent income, however, and no consensus on the best approach. In order to account for the differences in household size, Table 8 recalculates the first measure of income mobility using a relatively simple approach to measuring income mobility on an individual basis. In determining the number of households in each quintile, the tax returns of married couples filing jointly are counted as two individuals,

---

[31] Households with the same marital status in 1987 and 1996 may differ in various ways from those whose marital status changed. Some of these differences are likely to be correlated with income mobility. A more detailed examination of how incomes of individuals change after marriage or divorce is beyond the scope of this paper, but could be examined in future research.

[32] The top income quintile has more married couples and families with children, at least in part due to the presence of two wage earners in many households. The bottom income quintile is composed primarily of single individuals and single heads of households. Therefore, just as in fictional Lake Wobegon, well over half of the population is in a family with higher than average income. More than 20 percent of the people are in the top income quintile (as measured by households), and fewer than 20 percent of people are in the bottom 20 percent.

while all other types of returns (single, head of household, married filing separately, widowed) are counted as one individual. In determining the income cutoffs, the income of married couples is divided by two.

These adjustments have surprisingly little effect on measured income mobility. Measured mobility out of the bottom quintile is only about 4 percent lower, while downward mobility out of the top quintile is about 9 percent higher.

Table 8: Income Mobility with Adjustment for Family Size, Age 25 and Over, Relative to the Total Tax Filing Population, 1987-1996

1987 Income Quintile	1996 Income Quintile						Top 10%	Top 5%	Top 1%
	Lowest	Second	Middle	Fourth	Highest	Total			
Lowest	41.6	29.4	15.4	8.0	5.6	100.0	2.8	1.4	0.3
Second	18.6	33.8	26.5	14.7	6.4	100.0	2.2	1.1	0.2
Middle	8.5	20.6	32.0	26.8	12.2	100.0	4.1	1.4	0.3
Fourth	4.2	10.4	20.7	36.4	28.4	100.0	10.5	4.1	0.4
Highest	2.5	4.1	9.2	19.2	65.0	100.0	41.7	24.3	5.8
Top 10%	2.4	3.0	5.9	12.3	76.5	100.0	59.1	39.0	10.4
Top 5%	2.4	2.9	4.4	9.5	80.9	100.0	69.8	54.4	18.1
Top 1%	2.1	2.1	3.6	5.4	86.8	100.0	81.4	74.5	45.7
All	13.2	18.4	20.7	22.1	25.6	100.0	13.4	7.1	1.5

Source: U.S. Treasury Department, 1987-1996 Family Panel.
Notes: In this table returns of married couples filing jointly are counted as two persons for purposes of determining quintile population groups and the cash income of these households is divided by two for purposes of ranking households by income. The rows sum to 100 percent across the five quintiles in the first five columns. This table includes households who filed tax returns for both 1987 and 1996 where the primary taxpayer is age 25 or over in 1987. The income levels for the quintiles and top percentiles in 1987 and 1996 are determined using the full cross-sections of tax returns for 1987 and 1996 respectively, where the primary taxpayer is age 25 and over. Income is cash income as defined in the text and the technical and data appendix.

VII. Conclusions

This study presents an analysis of income mobility in the U.S. economy using a panel of individual income tax returns for 1987 and 1996. Two measures of relative income mobility are used to show how households' incomes change relative to the incomes of other households. A third mobility measure shows the absolute changes in households' real incomes over the sample period. The analysis illustrates the significant amount of income mobility in this time period.

More than half (57 percent) of households moved to a higher or lower income quintile between 1987 and 1996. Roughly half (61 percent by one measure and 45 percent by another) of the households in the lowest income quintile in 1987, had moved up to a higher income quintile by 1996. Over 7 percent raised their income sufficiently to enter the top income quintile by 1996. More importantly, households initially having the lowest incomes had the largest increases in real incomes. Nearly half of the households in the bottom income quintile at least doubled their real income over this period. Downward income mobility is more frequent among older households, likely reflecting transition to retirement. Much additional work needs to be done in this area, including more detailed examination of the factors contributing to upward and downward income mobility, extension to more recent periods, and the effects of taxes on after-tax incomes.

References

Ackerman, Deena, James Cilke, Julie-Anne Cronin, Janet Holtzblatt, Gillian Hunter, Emily Lin, Janet McCubbin and James R. Nunns. "Treasury's Panel Model for Tax Analysis," U.S. Department of the Treasury, OTA Paper, forthcoming 2007.

Bradbury, Katherine and Jane Katz. "Are Lifetime Incomes Growing More Unequal? Looking at New Evidence on Family Income Mobility" Regional Review, Q4, Federal Reserve Bank of Boston, September, 2002a.

_____. "Women's Labor Market Involvement and Family Income Mobility When Marriages End," New England Economic Review, No. 4, 2002b.

Burkhauser, Richard, Douglas Holtz-Eakin, and Stephen Rhody. "Labor Earnings Mobility and Inequality in the United States and Germany During the Growth Years of the 1980s," International Economic Review 38, No. 4, November 1997, 775-794.

Carroll, Robert, David Joulfaian and Mark Rider, "Income Mobility: The Recent American Experience," Andrew Young School of Policy Studies, Georgia State, Working Paper 06-20, July 2006

Cilke, James, Julie-Anne M. Cronin, Janet McCubbin, James R. Nunns, and Paul Smith. "Distributional Analysis: A Longer Term Perspective," in Proceedings of the Ninety-Third Annual Conference on Taxation, 248-258. Washington, D.C.: National Tax Association, 2001.

Congressional Budget Office. "Changes in the Economic Resources of Low-Income Households with Children," Congressional Budget Office Paper, May 2007.

Holtz-Eakin, Douglas, Harvey Rosen and Robert Weathers. "Horatio Alger Meets the Mobility Tables," Small Business Economics 14, No. 4, June 2000, 243-274.

McMurrer, Daniel and Isabel Sawhill. "Economic Mobility in the United States," No. 6722, Urban Institute, 1996a.

McMurrer, Daniel and Isabel Sawhill. "How Much Do Americans Move Up and Down the Economic Ladder?," in the Opportunity in America Series, No. 3. Washington, D.C.: Urban Institute November 1996b.

Piketty, Thomas and Emmanuel Saez, "Income Inequality in the United States, 1913-1998," Quarterly Journal of Economics, CXVIII, No. 1, February 2003.

Piketty, Thomas and Emmanuel Saez, "Income Inequality in the United States, Tables and Figures Updated to 2005", website: http://elsa.berkeley.edu/~saez/ , March 2007.

Sawhill, Isabel and Mark Condon. "Is U.S. Income Inequality Really Growing?: Sorting Out the Fairness Question," Policy Bites. Washington, D.C.: Urban Institute, 1992.

Sawhill, Isabel V., "Still the Land of Opportunity?," Urban Institute web site

U.S. Census Bureau. Income, Poverty, and Health Insurance Coverage in the United States, 2005, Current Population Reports P60-231. U.S. Government Printing Office, Washington, DC, 2006.

U.S. Treasury Department, Office of Tax Analysis. "Household Income Changes over Time: Some Basic Questions and Facts," Tax Notes 56, August 24, 1992a, 1065-1074.

U.S. Treasury Department, Office of Tax Analysis. "Household Income Mobility During the 1980s: A Statistical Assessment Based on Tax Return Data," Memo, June 1, 1992 (Also published as a Special Supplement in Tax Notes 55, June 1, 1992b.)

Appendix A: Technical and Data Appendix

Cash income is defined to include wages and salaries, tip income, taxable and tax-exempt interest, dividend income, alimony, net income from sole proprietorships, partnerships, and S corporations, farm income, net rental income, royalty income, net capital gain or loss in AGI, other gain or loss, unemployment compensation, taxable and non-taxable pension and annuity income, Social Security benefits (including the non-taxable portion), and other income included in AGI. Net operating losses carried over from prior years are added back. Disallowed passive losses and alimony paid are subtracted to reflect cash income. These sources of income are as reported on individual income tax returns and supplemented by data from information returns on Social Security benefits received but not subject to tax. The inclusion of tax-exempt interest and Social Security benefits are important improvements to income as generally measured on income tax returns. The inclusion of Social Security benefits is particularly important because it is the main source of income of many older households. As shown in the table below, transfer payments subject to tax and thus included in income tax return data accounted for about 86 percent of all cash transfer payments in 1995 (the closest available year to 1996). Thus, the income measure used in this study should generally provide a good measure of cash income.

Transfer Payments in the U.S, 1990 and 1995

Type of Transfer Payment	Millions of dollars		Percent of Transfers	
	1990	1995	1990	1995
Subject to income tax				
Old age, survivors & disability insurance benefits (Social Security)	244,135	327,667	74.2	75.2
Railroad retirement and disability benefits	7,221	8,028	2.2	1.8
Veterans pension and disability payments	7,775	8,782	2.3	2.0
Unemployment insurance benefits	17,644	21,838	5.4	5.0
Subtotal, payments subject to tax	284,550	375,098	84.2	84.0
Cash transfer payments not subject to income tax				
Worker's compensation payments	8,618	10,530	2.6	2.4
Supplemental Security Income (SSI)	16,670	27,726	5.1	6.4
Family assistance /1	19,187	22,637	5.8	5.2
Exempt Veterans disability payments	7,775	8,783	2.4	2.0
Subtotal, payments not subject to tax	44,475	60,893	13.5	14.0
Total cash transfer payments	329,025	435,991	100.0	100.0
Other transfer payments (generally in-kind	232,459	404,043		
Total transfer payments	561,484	840,034		

Source: U.S. Bureau of Economic Analysis, Regional Accounts Data, Table 527.
Note: The taxable portion of Veterans pension and disability payments is assumed to be 50 percent of the total.

For tax year 1987, the income thresholds at which taxpayers are required to file were $4,440 for single taxpayers and heads of households under age 65, and $7,560 for married couples filing jointly and both under age 65. For taxpayers age 65 and over, the thresholds were $5,650 for single taxpayers, $7,050 for heads of household, $9,400 for joint returns with one spouse age 65 or over and $10,000 for joint returns with both taxpayers age 65 and over. Other thresholds within this range applied in certain other cases. The higher thresholds for taxpayers age 65 and over and the exemption of Social Security benefits for lower income taxpayers means that a smaller percentage of the population age 65 and over file income tax returns. By tax year 1996, the income thresholds for taxpayers under age 65 increased to $6,550 for single taxpayers, $8,450 for heads of households, and $11,800 for married couples filing jointly. For taxpayers age 65 and over, the thresholds were $7,550 for single taxpayers, $9,450 for heads of household and $12,600 and $13,400 for joint returns with one and both spouses age 65 and over, respectively. The thresholds for married taxpayers filing separately were $1,500 in 1987 and $2,550 in 1996. While taxpayers with incomes under these thresholds were not required to file tax returns, many had an incentive to file in order obtain refunds of taxes withheld or the benefit of refundable tax credits such as the Earned Income Tax Credit.

Many of the tables in the text divide tax households into quintiles and also show households in the top 10 percent, 5 percent and 1 percent of households by income. The table below shows the income break points for these quintiles and percentiles.

Income Quintile or Percentile	Cash Income in Year	
	1987	1996
Lowest	Under 12,630	Under 15,861
Second	12,630	15,861
Middle	20,561	26,421
Fourth	30,289	39,441
Highest	44,952	61,270
Top 10%	59,987	85,961
Top 5%	78,873	118,362
Top 1%	175,181	290,724

Underreporting of income can be a problem for studies using income tax data as well as for studies using survey data. The table below shows the extent of underreporting in 1988 for each income quintile based on the 1988 Taxpayer Compliance Measurement Project (TCMP). Cash income as measured in this table does not include non-taxable Social Security benefits as these were not reported in the TCMP data. Overall about one-third of tax returns underreported total cash income. On those returns, total net unreported income was about 8.5 percent of reported cash income. In the lowest income quintile based on reported income, underreporting was less frequent (one-fourth of returns) but more severe on those returns as unreported income was 39 percent of reported income. Only 1.7 percent of returns (2.9 percent in the lowest income quintile had unreported income of 50 percent of reported income. When returns were categorized on the basis of post-audit corrected income, the differences in underreporting are less pronounced across income classes. Note that these data are not the same as the tax gap because tax rates are higher for high-income taxpayers, high-income taxpayers are more likely to have itemized deductions which may be overstated, and other technical aspects of tax gap estimates.

Underreporting of Income on Tax Returns in the 1988 TCMP

1988 Inome Quintile	Quintiles by reported income			Quintiles by corrected income		
	Percent of returns with underreported income	Unreported Income	Percent of returns with underreported income of 50 percent or more	Percent of returns with underreported income	Unreported Income	Percent of returns with underreported income of 50 percent or more
Lowest	25.2	39.1	2.9	30.4	16.7	6.7
Second	30.8	13.3	1.9	30.8	10.1	1.0
Middle	34.1	8.9	1.3	33.1	6.6	0.5
Fourth	37.3	7.3	1.0	36.0	5.2	0.2
Highest	42.6	7.7	1.4	39.6	4.6	0.2
Top 10%	45.9	7.9	1.8	41.8	4.4	0.2
Top 5%	49.9	8.2	2.7	45.8	4.2	0.2
Top 1%	53.2	6.2	2.0	50.1	3.7	0.2
All	34.0	8.5	1.7	34.0	8.5	1.7

Source: Tabulations by the authors from the 1988 Taxpayer Compliance Measurement Project (TCMP).
Notes: For the first three columns, income quintiles and percentiles are determined based on the cash income as reported on the taxpayer's return. For the last three columns, these are based on cash income as audited. Unreported income is shown as a percentage of reported income. For comparability to the current study, returns of dependent filers are excluded.

In order to examine how well the tax filing population represents the total population, the table below compares the age 20 and over taxpayer population to the U.S. resident population in 1987 by age group. The tax filing population in the table includes the primary taxpayer on all returns and the secondary taxpayer on joint returns of married couples. As with the panel used in the study, it does not include nearly 9 million dependent tax filers who are claimed as exemptions on another tax return. While most dependent taxpayers are age 23 or younger, a smaller number are elderly parents supported by their children or disabled adults.

The table shows that the tax filing population accounted for over 85 percent of the resident population aged 25 and over in 1987. Since the resident population includes the institutionalized population (prisons, nursing homes, etc), the proportion of the non-institutionalized population would be even higher. The tax filing population accounted for only 69 percent of the population aged 20 through 24 in 1987. This lower income tax filing rate reflects the fact that many in this age group are still full-time students and thus have reduced incomes and greater likelihood of being claimed as dependents for tax purposes. The filing rate also declines to 56 percent for individuals age 65 and over. The filing rate declines for this group because of lower incomes after retirement and also because of the tax treatment of Social Security benefits. Social Security benefits are not subject to tax unless modified adjusted gross income exceeds $25,000 for single persons and $35,000 for married couples. Thus, retired households whose income consists primarily of Social Security benefits do not need to file because their other income falls below the filing threshold.

Because the tax filing population is less representative of the full population of younger individuals and households, the analysis generally excludes taxpayers under age 25. Some tables also exclude taxpayers who are age 65 and over by the end of the time period in the analysis. The tax file accounted for 92.5 percent of the resident population age 25 to 64 in 1987.

Comparison of the Adult Tax Filing Population with the U.S. Resident Population, 1987

Age group	Tax Filing Population			U.S Resident Population			Tax population as percent of resident population		
	Men	Women	Total	Men	Women	Total	Men	Women	Total
20-24	7,065	7,050	14,115	10,339	10,104	20,442	68.3	69.8	69.0
25-64	54,473	57,539	112,012	59,301	61,770	121,071	91.9	93.2	92.5
65 and over	7,612	8,821	16,432	11,779	17,568	29,346	64.6	50.2	56.0
25 and over	62,085	66,360	128,445	71,079	79,338	150,417	87.3	83.6	85.4

Sources: U.S. Treasury Department, 1987-1996 Family Panel and U.S. Bureau of the Census, Resident Population Estimates for January 1, 1987.
Notes: Population numbers are in thousands.

Another important aspect of the use of panels is attrition over time. As a result, the size of panels tends to decline over time. The table below shows information on attrition in the panel for 1987 and 1996. Note that this table includes tax households where the primary taxpayer is under age 65 that are excluded from most analysis in the study.

Attrition in the 1987-1996 Treasury Panel by Income Class and Age

1987 Income Quintile	Numbers of Non-dependent Tax Units (weighted units are in thousands)					Percent Attrition from 1987 Sample			
	1987 Sample	Died	Other attrition, age 65 and over	Other attrition, under age 65	1996 Sample	Died	Other attrition, age 65 and over	Other attrition, under age 65	1996 Sample
Lowest	9,620	459	326	1,396	7,439	4.8	3.4	14.5	22.7
Second	6,690	591	570	745	4,784	8.8	8.5	11.1	28.5
Middle	7,393	823	533	507	5,530	11.1	7.2	6.9	25.2
Fourth	9,394	856	315	403	7,820	9.1	3.4	4.3	16.8
Highest	54,801	4,258	644	1,350	48,549	7.8	1.2	2.5	11.4
All	87,898	6,987	2,388	4,401	74,122	7.9	2.7	5.0	15.7
Weighted									
Lowest	14,878	581	575	2,939	10,783	3.9	3.9	19.8	27.5
Second	16,443	1,463	1,417	1,897	11,667	8.9	8.6	11.5	29.0
Middle	18,030	2,038	1,339	1,286	13,368	11.3	7.4	7.1	25.9
Fourth	19,173	1,954	716	865	15,639	10.2	3.7	4.5	18.4
Highest	29,238	2,227	392	735	25,885	7.6	1.3	2.5	11.5
All	97,762	8,262	4,438	7,721	77,341	8.5	4.5	7.9	20.9

Sources: U.S. Treasury Department, 1987-1996 Family Panel.
Notes: This table includes tax households where the primary taxpayer is under age 65 that are not included in the study. Since these taxpayers have a higher attrition rate than taxpayers age 25 to 64, this table overstates the attrition rate somewhat.

As shown in the table, about 8 percent of the tax households present in 1987 are no longer in the sample by 1996 because the primary taxpayer has died. An additional 7.7 percent of the tax households are no longer in the sample for other reasons, resulting in a total attrition rate of 15.7 percent. Among the reasons why taxpayers do not file in the later year are declines in income so that the taxpayer falls below the tax filing threshold, retires and receives Social Security benefits rather than taxable wages (Social Security benefits are not taxable for lower-income households), files very late (late filers up to two years late are included), emigrates to another country, dies but the death is not recorded in the tax records. More than one-third (35 percent) of the attrition other than death was among taxpayers age 65 or over by 1996. The non-filing status of this group largely reflects the non-taxability of Social Security benefits except for the less than one-fifth of taxpayers with Social Security benefits with total incomes over certain income thresholds and may or may not reflect a decline in cash income.

Appendix B: Results of Prior Studies

This appendix reproduces tables from several prior studies of income mobility that are discussed in the text of this paper. These studies differ in the time periods covered, the measures of income used, age or other limits placed on the sample examined and other features. In addition, the second table is approximately reproduces the Sawhill and Condon methodology using the data used in the current study.

Sawhill and Condon (1992): Distribution Across Income Quintiles in 1986 of Families with Members Aged 25-54 in 1977 by the Income Quintile the Family was in in 1977

1977 Income Quintile	1986 Income Quintile					
	Lowest	Second	Middle	Fourth	Highest	Total
Lowest	53	25	11	7	4	100
Second	22	30	26	15	9	100
Middle	15	19	30	24	13	100
Fourth	5	15	22	34	25	100
Highest	6	11	13	21	50	100
All	20	20	20	20	20	100

Source: Sawhill and Condon (1992) Table 1, as reproduced in U.S. Treasury (1992b).
Notes: Based on data from PSID. Numbers were rescaled in U.S. Treasury (1992b) to add to 100 for each 1977 quintile by multiplying the original numbers by 5.

For comparison purposes, the following table uses the Family Panel data from the current study, but uses the mobility measure and imposes age limits closely approximating the Sawhill and Condon (1992) table.

Sawhill and Condon (1992) Methodology Using the Family Panel for 1987-1996.

1987 Income Quintile	1996 Income Quintile					
	Lowest	Second	Middle	Fourth	Highest	Total
Lowest	54	23	11	7	5	100
Second	25	37	21	12	6	100
Middle	12	24	32	21	11	100
Fourth	5	12	26	37	20	100
Highest	3	5	11	23	58	100
All	3	3	7	15	73	100

Source: Calculated using the 1987-1996 Family Panel.
Notes: Table includes tax households with primary taxpayers age 25 to 55 in 1987.
This table compares the same households based on categorizing them first on their 1987 income and then on their 1996 income.

Bradbury and Katz (2002b) Family Income Mobility Patterns, All Families

1988 Income Quintile	1998 Income Quintile					
	Lowest	Second	Middle	Fourth	Highest	Total
Lowest	53.3	23.6	12.4	6.4	4.3	100.0
Second	25.7	36.3	22.6	11.0	4.3	100.0
Middle	10.9	20.7	28.3	27.5	12.6	100.0
Fourth	6.5	12.9	23.7	31.1	25.8	100.0
Highest	3.0	5.7	14.9	23.2	53.2	100.0
All	20.0	20.0	20.0	20.0	20.0	100.0

Source: Bradbury and Katz (2002b), Appendix A.
Notes: Based on data from PSID. Excludes families with no primary person age 65 or under, but no lower age bound is imposed.

US Treasury (1992b) Distribution Across 1988 Income Quintiles of Taxpayers Grouped by Their 1979 Income Quintiles.

1979 Income Quintile	1988 Income Quintile					
	Lowest	Second	Middle	Fourth	Highest	Total
Lowest	14	21	25	25	15	100
Second	11	29	30	20	11	100
Middle	6	14	33	32	15	100
Fourth	3	9	15	38	35	100
Highest	1	4	9	20	65	100
All	20	20	20	20	20	100

Source: Table 1 in U.S. Treasury (1992b).
Notes: The income breaks for determining the 1979 and 1988 income quintiles are based on the full cross-sections of tax returns filed in those years.